ZINC

A TRUE BOOK®

by

Salvatore Tocci

Children's Press®
A Division of Scholastic Inc.

New York Toronto London Auckland Sydney
Mexico City New Delhi Hong Kong
Danbury, Connecticut

The batteries of most laptop computers are made of zinc.

Reading Consultant
Julia McKenzie Munemo, MEd
New York, New York

Science Consultant
John A. Benner
Austin, Texas

The photo on the cover shows a sample of zinc. The photo on the title page shows smithsonite, an ore of zinc.

The author and the publisher are not responsible for injuries or accidents that occur during or from any experiments. Experiments should be conducted in the presence of or with the help of an adult. Any instructions of the experiments that require the use of sharp, hot, or other unsafe items should be conducted by or with the help of an adult.

Library of Congress Cataloging-in-Publication Data

Tocci, Salvatore.
    Zinc / by Salvatore Tocci.
        p. cm. — (A true book)
    Includes bibliographical references and index.
    ISBN 0-516-23703-9 (lib. bdg.)   0-516-25579-7 (pbk.)
    1. Zinc—Juvenile literature. I. Title. II. Series.
QD181.Z6T58 2005
546'.661—dc22   2004027151

Contents

Have you ever shared one of your favorite foods with a friend at lunchtime?

Have You Ever Made a Sacrifice?

Have you ever given up something without getting anything in return? Although you may not have realized it, you made a sacrifice. Perhaps you made a sacrifice by going without dessert at lunch one day because you gave it to a friend.

Or you may have made a sacrifice by agreeing to watch your friend's favorite television show instead of your own.

People who own boats also make sacrifices of a sort. Boaters sacrifice a piece of zinc metal. Metal objects on the bottom of a boat, such as the propeller, **corrode** quickly in salt water. To prevent corrosion, boaters attach a tiny piece of zinc metal to the shaft that runs from the engine to

The piece of zinc metal that is attached to the propeller shaft must be replaced when it has corroded.

the propeller. This helps prevent the propeller from
becoming corroded because
the zinc metal corrodes
before the propeller can. In
other words, this tiny piece
of zinc metal is sacrificed to
save the much more valuable
and important steel propeller.
The boat owner should check
to make sure the zinc has
not corroded. As long as the
zinc is there, the propeller
will not corrode.

Can you see the tiny gas bubbles that are formed as the zinc reacts with the vinegar?

What Is Zinc?

Zinc is an **element**. An element is one of the building blocks of **matter**. Matter is the stuff or material that makes up everything in the universe. This book, the chair you are sitting on, and even your body are all made of matter.

There are millions of different kinds of matter. However, there are just a few more than one hundred different elements. How can so many different kinds of matter be made up of so few elements?

Think about the English language. Just twenty-six letters can be arranged to make up all the words in the language. Likewise, the one hundred elements can be arranged to make up all the different kinds of matter in the universe.

Every ton of Earth's crust contains about 2.3 ounces (65 grams) of zinc.

Some metals are very active. This means that they will easily react with other substances.

Every ton of Earth's crust contains about 2.3 ounces (65 grams) of zinc.

Some metals are very active. This means that they will easily react with other substances.

Can you see the tiny gas bubbles that are formed as the zinc reacts with the vinegar?

For example, if you put a piece of zinc in a glass of vinegar, tiny gas bubbles will slowly appear and rise to the surface. The bubbles show that the zinc is reacting with the vinegar.

The more active a metal is, the more likely it is to corrode. Zinc is more active than iron, which is a metal used to make steel. Therefore, zinc will corrode before steel does when both metals are exposed to salt water.

Exposing the Zinc

Pennies are made by coating a round piece of zinc metal with a thin layer of copper. Try this experiment. Use a file to carefully remove the copper layer from around the edge of a penny. The shiny metal that appears is zinc. Place the penny in a glass or jar so that it leans against the side. Slowly pour vinegar into the glass so that the penny is covered.

Each day, watch what happens to the penny. When all the zinc has been used up, the copper that remains may float to the top. Even though zinc is an active metal, it may take a couple of weeks before all the zinc is gone.

How Else Is Zinc Useful?

Besides protecting expensive boat parts, zinc is useful in other ways. One of its main uses is in a process known as **galvanization**. This process involves using zinc to coat an object that is likely to corrode.

Galvanization is commonly used for coating iron nails. The more zinc used to coat the iron nail, the longer it will take for the nail to rust. Even galvanized nails will rust, however, once all the zinc has corroded and exposed the iron.

Zinc is also used to make batteries, including those that power flashlights. The batteries provide the electricity to

Zinc is used to make the part of the battery that is marked with the negative (−) sign.

light up the bulb. As electricity flows through the bulb, a thin wire gets hot enough to give off light.

Making a Battery

Wrap the end of a piece of copper wire around a galvanized nail. Wrap another piece of wire around a penny. Stick the nail and penny into a large, juicy lemon. Make sure that the nail and penny do not touch. Touch the wire from the nail to one of the wires on a light-emitting diode (LED), which you can purchase at an electronics store. Touch the wire from the copper penny to the other wire on the LED. The LED should glow. The zinc on the galvanized nail helps the lemon to work like a battery. Experiment to see what else will work besides a lemon. You can try an orange, a tomato, and a potato.

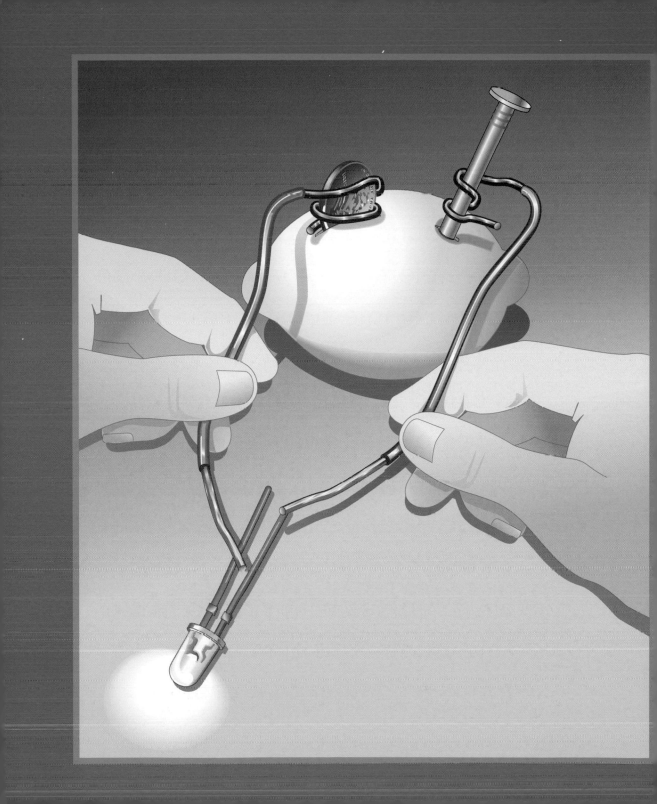

Some **compounds** that contain zinc are also useful. A compound is made of two or more elements that combine to form a single substance.

One useful zinc compound is called zinc oxide, which is made of zinc and the element oxygen. This compound is made whenever zinc is exposed to the air. The oxygen in the air combines with zinc to make zinc oxide. This zinc oxide forms a coating that protects

When iron is exposed to moisture and air, the iron breaks down and rust forms.

the zinc underneath from corroding. This coating helps prevent galvanized nails from rusting.

This beachgoer wears a cream that contains zinc oxide. It protects his nose and lips from the damaging rays of the sun.

Zinc oxide has many other uses. It is an ingredient in some sunscreens. It is also sold as a pigment for artists called zinc white.

The rubber industry is a major user of zinc oxide. It is used to help speed up the process of making rubber for tires. It also helps prevent rubber tires from being easily damaged by heat. This is important because when

Zinc oxide is used to make truck tires (above) and other kinds of tires.

cars and trucks travel at high speeds, **friction** between tires and the road causes the tires to get hot.

Zinc oxide is also added to animal feed. Without zinc in their diets, many animals would become ill and fail to grow properly. The same is true for humans, though they need only a very tiny amount of zinc in their diets. A well-balanced diet that includes

People can get all the zinc their bodies need by eating foods such as meat, eggs, and dairy products.

meat, fish, and dairy products provides all the zinc a person needs.

Taking in too much zinc, however, can be harmful. A high level of zinc can prevent another element called copper from being absorbed by the human body. Like zinc, people need copper to stay healthy.

What Are Zinc Alloys?

In 1787, the U.S. government started minting pennies made of pure copper. In time, making the coin cost more than the penny was worth. As a result, in 1982, the government started using less copper in its pennies. Today, a penny is only 2.5 percent copper. The remaining

These pennies are
made mostly of zinc.

97.5 percent of the penny is zinc. Together, zinc and copper make up an **alloy**.

An alloy is made by mixing a metal with one or more other elements. An alloy is different from a compound. In an alloy, the elements are mixed together and can be easily separated from one another. In a compound, the elements are combined and cannot be easily separated.

To understand the difference between an alloy and a compound, imagine that you are making a cheese omelet. When you mix the eggs and cheese in a bowl, you have a mixture. You can still separate the cheese from the eggs. A cooked omelet, however, represents a compound. The eggs and cheese have been combined so that you cannot separate them easily.

Brass is a zinc alloy with a long history. It was used long before zinc was discovered as an element. Scientists did not isolate zinc as an element until the mid-1700s. Until then, there was no way of heating metal ores to the very high temperatures needed to separate the pure zinc.

The ancient Greeks and Romans first used brass about two thousand years ago. The copper in brass gave this zinc

Brass is sometimes used to make buttons.

alloy a golden color that people liked. The Romans used brass to make helmets for soldiers and jewelry for women.

In the 1800s, a method was invented to make large, brass sheets at a reasonable cost. Until that time, copper sheets had been used to cover the hulls of wooden ships. This metal protected the ship from being slowly destroyed by worms and other small animals.

Brass was used to make shells for the explosives fired by this World War II artillery gun.

Copper, however, was expensive. Shipbuilders found brass did the same job at a lower cost. Today, people use brass to make faucets, musical instruments, lamps, door handles, locks, hinges, screws, and buttons for clothes.

Another useful zinc alloy is **solder**. Solder is used to join metal parts. Metalworkers hold the solder against the metal parts and heat it to its melting point. As the solder cools, it turns back into a solid and forms a strong bond between the metal parts.

A zinc alloy is also used to make a variety of kitchen utensils. These include bottle and can openers, ladles, potato mashers, pastry cutters, ice cream scoops, garlic presses, and pizza cutters. The zinc alloy makes these utensils sturdy and less likely to corrode.

This zinc butter cooler was
made in the late 1800s.

Zinc protects a variety of household items as well as the metal parts of boats from corroding. This important element improves your life in many ways you probably never thought about before.

Fun Facts About Zinc

- Zinc is the fourth-most used metal in the United States. The first three are iron, aluminum, and copper.

- For more than two hundred years, people in Europe have covered their roofs with sheets of zinc. A zinc roof has a life span of at least sixty years compared to the fifteen-year life span of a shingled roof.

- About 17 pounds (8 kilograms) of zinc are used to protect the steel on an automobile from rusting.

- The tires on a car contain about 2 pounds (1 kg) of zinc.

- A zinc battery can power a laptop computer for more than twelve hours.

- Zinc batteries can store six times more energy per pound than other types of batteries.

- Galvanization with zinc has greatly reduced the cost of replacing metals that have corroded. Even so, corrosion is still estimated to cost more than $200 billion each year in the United States alone.

- The Alaskan oil pipeline is protected from corrosion by a zinc cable that runs the entire length of the pipeline.

- More than one-third of the zinc used in the United States is recovered from old cars, bridges, and buildings.

To Find Out More

To learn more about zinc, check out these additional sources.

 **Books**

Krasnow, David, and Tom Seddon. **Elements**. Gareth Stevens, 2003.

Oxlade, Chris. **Elements & Compounds.** Heinemann Library, 2002.

Stille, Darlene, **Minerals: From Apatite to Zinc.** Compass Point, 2005.

Stwertka, Albert. **A Guide to Elements.** Oxford University Press, 1996.

Tocci, Salvatore. **The Periodic Table.** Children's Press, 2004.

Organizations and Online Sites

American Zinc Association
2025 M Street NW
Suite 800
Washington, DC 20036
http://www.zinc.org

Learn all you ever wanted to know about how zinc is used. You can also download educational videos about zinc.

It's Elemental
http://education.jlab.org/ itselemental/ele030.html

Visit this site for information about the history and uses of zinc. You can read about zinc compounds, such as zinc sulfide, which is used in television screens.

A Potato Battery
http://www.physlink.com/ Education/AskExperts/ ae516.cfm

Find out how you can make a battery with zinc, copper, and a potato. You can also learn more about how zinc helps electricity flow to light up a bulb.

The History of Brass
http://www.brass.org/ history.htm

Learn what the Greeks and Romans called brass and how they used it. Read about how the clock used to determine longitude was made in 1761 with the help of brass.

Important Words

alloy substance made by mixing a metal with one or more other substances

compound substance formed from the combination of two or more elements

corrode wear away slowly as a result of a chemical process

element building block of matter

friction force created when two objects rub against each other

galvanization process of coating one metal with another metal

matter stuff or material that makes up everything in the universe

solder alloy that is used to join metal parts

Index

Meet the Author

Salvatore Tocci is a science writer who lives in East Hampton, New York, with his wife, Patti. He was a high school biology and chemistry teacher for almost thirty years. His books include a high school chemistry textbook and an elementary school book series that encourages students to perform experiments to learn about science. Every year, Mr. Tocci and his wife place a piece of zinc metal on the propeller shaft before their sailboat is launched.